F.A.I.T.H.
FORSAKING ALL I TRUST HIM

REGINA PRICE

F.A.I.T.H. – Forsaking All I Trust Him

F.A.I.T.H. – Forsaking All I Trust Him
Copyright © 2017 by Regina Price

All rights reserved.
No parts of this book may be reproduced in any form or by any electronic or mechanical means including information storage and retrieval systems, without the prior written permission of the publisher, with the exception of brief excerpts used for the purpose of review. No adaptation of the material in this book may be used for stage, television, film, radio, or any other performance unless written authorization has been obtained from the author.

Printed in the United States of America.

ISBN: 978069292481-5

Book Designed by: SmallBizNiz.com

Foreword & Editing by: Pastors Sean and Kim Walsh

*Unless otherwise noted all Scripture quotations are taken from:

King James Version.
The New King James Version. Copyright© 1982 by Thomas Nelson, Inc. Used by permission. All rights reserved.
The Student Bible; New International Version® Copyright© 1986,1992,1996 by The Zondervan Corporation. Used by permission of Zondervan. All rights reserved.
Amplified Bible (AMP). Copyright© 2015 by The Lockman Foundation. La Habra, CA 90631. All rights reserved.
The New American Standard Bible. 1960, 1962, 1963, 1968, 1971, 1972, 1973, 1975, 1977, 1995 by The Lockman Foundation. Used by permission of Lockman Foundation. All rights reserved.

For information visit: **www.alite4life.com**

TABLE OF CONTENTS

Acknowledgments .... iv.

Foreword .... vi.

Endorsements .... vii.

About The Author .... ix.

F.A.I.T.H.

The Journey Begins .... Page - 11

Introduction – Faith Shift .... Page - 23

Chapter 1 – Forsaking .... Page - 34

Chapter 2 – All .... Page - 39

Chapter 3 – I .... Page - 44

Chapter 4 – Trust .... Page - 50

Chapter 5 – Him .... Page - 55

Conclusion .... Page - 60

Salvation Prayer .... Page - 64

F.A.I.T.H. Prayer .... Page - 65

Understanding and Conquering ACEs .... Page - 66

My F.A.I.T.H. Journal .... Page - 78

F.A.I.T.H. – Forsaking All I Trust Him

ACKNOWLEDGMENTS

First and Foremost, I would like to thank my Lord and Savior Jesus Christ, for the inspiration to write this book and HIS precious Holy Spirit for guidance, wisdom, strength and power to carry it through. To HIM belong all the glory, honor and praise! Through this process I have realized that "I can do all things through Christ who strengthens me" (Philippians 4:13). What an honor to continually educate, encourage and empower others all over the world. To my loving family, Godmother and some of the dearest friends a girl could ever have, those of you who believed in me and supported me along this journey, I say "THANK YOU!" - Even to those who didn't believe because you motivated me to endure to the end.

I would like to personally thank professional author, speaker, coach and film director "Ari Squires" for encouraging me to "release the chains" at her 2014 Release the Chains Life Class Experience for Women. The call to write this book was prophesied over my life many years ago but I didn't receive the inspiration and motivation until I attended Release the Chains! This empowerment class equipped me to reclaim my life's purpose and destiny while reminding me that everything I need to succeed is already within me. Thank you Ari Squires! I

REGINA PRICE

would like to thank God for a precious gift in my life, my Pastors Fred and Inger Wyatt, who taught me that whatever I do, don't lose HOPE, because I am a HOPE GIVER. I also acknowledge my sister, friend and #1 supporter Melissa Parks, my good friends, Ministers Ray and Janice Harper for their endorsement of this book, my foreword and editors Pastors Sean and Kim Walsh, Ultimate Life Ministries, Fredericksburg, Virginia for all the encouraging words and support to see this dream become a reality.

F.A.I.T.H. – Forsaking All I Trust Him

FOREWORD

As pastors for over twelve years, we've had the privilege to watch Regina Price both walk out and mature in her faith journey. During this time we have never seen her try to "jockey" for a position in ministry or make a name for herself. Instead we have watched her serve God, her family, church and community both humbly and faithfully. Even though we are no longer her pastors, we are still honored to call her friend!

Adrian Rogers said, "A faith that hasn't been tested cant' be trusted." We know that Regina's faith has been tested far beyond what she has shared in this book and we can, without reservation, say that you can trust her!

This book speaks to Regina's real-life faith journey and some of its challenges and triumphs. It speaks to the need we all have to put our whole-hearted trust and faith in God and helps us learn how to do that unconditionally. We know you will be encouraged, inspired, challenged and empowered to step out in FAITH and go after everything God has called you to do.

Sean & Kim Walsh
Ultimate Life Ministries, Fredericksburg, Virginia

REGINA PRICE
ENDORSEMENTS

It is with great pleasure and honor to reflect on my dear Friend and Sister Regina Price, a woman of Great Faith. Regina is my older sibling with a difference of one year between us. She has no biological children of her own yet a mother to many. We share in common my son, J'haun who is one of her four God-children.

Since childhood my sister has always possessed a deep love for the Lord and would often ensure on Saturdays that she would be attending church on Sundays, starting with Sunday School. As years went by her love grew even stronger and she begin at an early age to "Walk by Faith, and not by Sight"!

She is often setting goals, stepping out on Faith and trusting God to hold her hand as she walks with self-assurance that nothing is impossible. Regina is a strong pillar in our family and always reminds us to have FAITH in every situation and Trust God in all that we do!

I'm truly blessed to have her as a sister and a friend, I've learned a great deal from her. We often shared laughs as she worked diligently to achieve her education, she would always state how challenging it was and the need for much prayer during the semesters, yet she would Ace it every time.

She recently took a leap of Faith and relocated to Richmond, Va. and God has opened so many doors and continuously has her in awe of all that he is unveiling right before her eyes. I'm in great anticipation and on the edge of my seat patiently waiting the arrival of this book "Forsaking All I Trust Him". Many will be blessed, inspired, and motivated after reading this book.

Majestic Entrepreneur!
Melissa Parks
Fredericksburg, Virginia

F.A.I.T.H. – Forsaking All I Trust Him

Regina Price and my family met through a mutual friend over twenty years ago. Regina had not yet received the baptism of the Holy Spirit and was wondering what that experience was all about, and was it really necessary. We didn't offer her any large explanations about the Holy Spirit, but simply prayed that the LORD would do the work.

One Sunday, while visiting the church Regina attended, an Altar Call was made. Regina and I both went up for prayer. As we were standing together praying, I began to hear a language coming from her that was not English. The LORD had baptized her in the Holy Spirit, with the evidence of speaking in tongues.

I knew then that her life would never be the same. And it hasn't. A few years after that experience, Regina revealed to us that the LORD was leading her to leave the area to attend a Bible College in Ohio. We all realized this would be a defining moment in her life.

Would she be able to let go of everything and everyone she held dear to follow the leading of the LORD to a place she had never been? Regina did indeed leave family and friends, sold her possessions and moved forward, listening to the voice that promised to "never leave nor forsake her." This book, Forsaking All I Trust Him, is birthed out of a spiritual journey that still continues, and will serve as a source of encouragement to those whose hearts are set on pilgrimage.

Watching how the LORD has manifested Himself through Regina, and her willingness to follow his leading, has inspired many, my family included, to truly trust and depend on GOD! We are so honored that the LORD allows us to be a part of her life, and to be numbered among her friends.

Joy!

Ministers Raymond & Janice Harper
Fredericksburg, Virginia

REGINA PRICE
ABOUT THE AUTHOR

Romans 8:28 says "And we know that all things work together to the good of them that love God to them that are the called according to his purpose." KJV

It's not just the good things or the bad things but Regina Price understands that **All** of life's experiences are working for her good because she is called by God. At the age of six, Regina professed the Lord Jesus Christ as her personal Savior and was baptized at the Macedonia Baptist Church, Woodford, Virginia. Regina didn't have full revelation knowledge of how much her Father, God, loved her and spent most of her young adult years looking for love in all the wrong places. This led to early challenges with drugs, alcohol and sexual immorality. Regina is familiar with the "Troubles of Life" and she has learned firsthand that having "Faith" will see you through any obstacle.

Regina re-dedicated her life to the Lord Jesus Christ on June 9, 1996 and in 1998, accepted the call by God to preach the Gospel of Jesus. After intensive counseling and training, she was licensed on March 5, 2000 at the Macedonia Baptist Church and served as a youth minister. In 2001 Regina received a prophetic word from the Lord to relocate to Columbus, OH and attend World Harvest Bible College now Valor Christian College and graduated with a Diploma in Pastoral and General Church Leadership in May 2005.

She facilitated Bible study and life skills classes at the Rappahannock Regional jail, Stafford, Virginia for nine years and worked alongside author, motivational speaker, and prison re-entry advocate

F.A.I.T.H. - Forsaking All I Trust Him

Lisa Kratz Thomas. Lisa is the former owner and operator of New Vision, a nonprofit reentry organization assisting the returning citizen transition from prison to purpose. Regina has continued to transform lives through her partnership with the Rappahannock Area Office on Youth to facilitate Restorative Justice Classes to Juvenile Offenders, Offender Aid and Restoration (OAR) of Richmond, Virginia to facilitate anger management classes at Richmond City Justice Center, and Bible study at the Bon Air Juvenile Correctional Facility in Chesterfield, Virginia. Regina received a certificate in Evangelism from The Way of the Master Biblical School of Evangelism in 2017 and is honored to serve as a co-laborer and Overseer of Evangelism at Speaking Spirit Ministries, Richmond, VA under the visionaries and leadership of her Pastors Fred and Inger Wyatt.

Regina is a mentor, coach, friend and advocate for children, women and returning citizens and has changed the trajectory of countless children lives for the better forever through her nine years of employment with the Rappahannock Big Brothers Big Sisters, a one-to-one mentor organization that pairs mentors with mentees. She is the proud godmother of four amazing young adults, J'haun, India, Ciera and Jada. Regina received her undergraduate degree from Strayer University in Business Administration with a Concentration in Management in 2008 and a Master of Education in 2015.

REGINA PRICE

THE JOURNEY BEGINS

"P" is what they called her! She had big brown "Popeyes" and ponytails. "P" was only four years old but she can vividly remember everything as if it was yesterday. She was living in Washington, D.C. with her father, mother and youngest sister. "P's" mother wasn't too thrilled about raising her family in the District of Columbia so they loaded up the car and moved back to the country, *Caroline County, VA* to join up with "P's" two older sisters who were residing with other relatives during that time. Both "P's" dad and mom's jobs had relocated them to D.C. but now it was time to go because "P" would be starting Pre-Kindergarten and a new baby brother was soon to come. Back then it was a privilege to attend Pre-K because it wasn't offered prevalently as it is in the school system today. "P" was so excited about going to school! In Pre-K she learned all the basics and more that prepared her for Kindergarten and First grade and she was actually a smart little girl who loved to read and received countless recognition from her Pre-K teacher for all her accomplishments and achievements.

Growing up in the country computers, cell phones and cable T.V. were virtually non-existent so "P", her siblings and cousins always created their own fun and games. "P's" mother had seven sisters and two brothers and they always came together at one of their homes to eat, play cards, listen to music, dance and have family fun. It was absolutely unheard of for children to be amongst grown-up conversations and entertainment so when the meal wrapped up they knew it was their cue to go outside and play. "P", her siblings and cousins didn't mind;

F.A.I.T.H. – Forsaking All I Trust Him

they actually looked forward to playing outside. They made swings from trees using tire inner tubes, found old furniture to decorate their club houses in the woods, played hide-n-go seek, marbles, hopscotch, Simon Says, 1-2-3 red light and so many more of those traditional children's games. The kids today don't have a clue about *"creative fun"* due to all the modern day technology and social media.

Snow days generally meant there was no school due to the icy country roads so they would gather together to play board and card games such as spades and Pokeno. Walking to Rozell's, the neighborhood country store, was the highlight of all! They would layer up with two and three pairs of socks on their feet, boots, coat, a hat and scarf and - when there were no gloves - socks served the purpose to warm their hands. The most important family activity of all that "P" looked forward to every week was Sunday school and church service on Sunday mornings. She was so excited about going that she would start preparing herself on Saturday evening. "P's" siblings called her a "holy-roller" because they didn't want to go to church as often as she did, but this didn't stop "P" she would burst into tears if she was told she couldn't go to church. Little did she know this was just the beginning of her **Faith** walk and love for God.

I'll tell you a secret about "P", she was known as the *"spoiled one"* of the family. I'm sure some of you can relate to this, you've probably earned the t-shirt and worn it well. "P's" father used to say, "she is just like my momma" and those words were sentimental to him because "P" reminded him so much of his momma and for that *"boo and pootie-rat"* as he called her could do no wrong in her daddy's eyes!

On the other hand, "P's" mother was a Proverbs 13:24 woman believing, **"whoever spares the rod hates their children, but the one who loves their children is careful to discipline them."** Whenever "P" deserved a good ole' butt whipping her mother didn't hesitate to give it to her but if daddy was around he would say, *"Leave boo alone."* Well, this didn't sit too well with her siblings so there was always a rivalry or a settling of a score to be had and whenever "P's" parents would leave to go hang out with family and friends, "P" and her siblings did things they were told not to do. Many times "P's" siblings would lock her in the closet so she couldn't participate in their activities because when she did participate, she would wait until their parents returned home and tell *"dear dad and mom"* everything!

Yikes! "P's" daddy would then turn into the Proverbs 13:24 father and her siblings would get the beat down! Boy, were there ever some consequences to pay for being a tattletale! "P" was beaten, scared with a rubber snake, called names, threatened - whatever punishments her siblings believed were necessary was how they evened the score! Those were the days! "P" knew her siblings loved her; they just didn't like her because she was a tattletale and a daddy's girl all because, "she looks just like my momma!" Growing up certainly had its challenges like most families do, times were tough back then and finances were limited too. "P's" mother was a hard-worker and did the very best she could raising six children because *"Ole Poppa"* was a rolling stone! He kept the wheels on the car shining and rolling, rolling, rolling, rolling, rolling on a river! He would shine those shoes, put on what we called his glad rags and tell "P's" mother, "I will be back in about an hour or an hour and a half" which would turn into days or weeks but that was still *"Ole Poppa"!*

"P" learned at an early age that the women back then were not only faithful but also committed to their husbands and the father of their children for sure! It didn't matter what they went through, they hung in there and worked it out even if that meant fighting it out or arguing their point by any means necessary and then making up as if nothing ever happened. It's called sweeping the dirt under the rug. Now that was really strange to "P", all she knew was something was very wrong about that picture and if that was how life was to be lived and relationships were to be experienced she wanted no part of it. Thank God that some children are pretty resilient and can bounce right back from traumatic situations; others suffer from something called Adverse Childhood Experiences (ACEs), potentially traumatic events that can have a negative, lasting effect on a person's health and well-being. These experiences range from physical, emotional, or sexual abuse to parental divorce, domestic violence or the incarceration of a parent or guardian.

Studies show that adults who experienced ACEs adopt health risk behaviors as coping mechanisms (e.g., eating disorders, smoking, substance abuse, self-harm, sexual promiscuity). There are also added medical conditions for those suffering with ACEs such as heart disease, pulmonary disease, liver disease, STDs and gynecologic cancer as well as early death (*Felitti et al,* 1998). So while a child may appear to be normal the release of profound anguish and anxiety, due to these ACEs can overtake their minds. This can manifest in uncontrollable anger and outbursts, depression, stress, anxiety and attention seeking.

"P" learned that her parents exhibited some ACEs of their own —divorce, alcohol abuse and domestic violence had been passed down in "P's" family. I'm sure some of you can relate to this. The Bible speaks of the *"Sins of the Father"*, **"Keeping mercy for thousands, forgiving iniquity and transgression and sin, and that will by no means clear [the guilty]; visiting the iniquity of the fathers upon the children, and upon the children's children, unto the third and to the fourth generation (Exodus 34:17).** Not only can sickness and disease, such as cancer, diabetes and high blood pressure be passed down through the bloodline but the model of sin that you see will be passed down for future generations until you receive knowledge of something different. "P" can remember the anxiety and stress she felt when *"Ole Poppa's"* car would pull up in the driveway after he had been gone for days. She knew that something was about to "pop off" because "P's" mother was certainly not a push over. "P" would sometimes run to greet daddy because just as she could do no wrong in his eye, he could do no wrong in her eyes. However, this didn't sit too well with "P's" mother and it increased her aggravation at *"Ole Poppa"* for his absence. Her interrogation and his famous words, "I was over the country" led from one thing to another and it was on and Poppin! "P" decided she was not leaving the home in the midst of her mother and father's disputes. She was a peacemaker, **"Blessed are the peacemakers, for they will be called children of God" (Matthew 5:9)** and was not about to see her mother and father hurt one another.

Surely, there were times that "P" could have been injured in

F.A.I.T.H. - Forsaking All I Trust Him

the midst of all the chaos but she had the spirit of a "Bulldog", full of tenacity and strength. When she put her mind to something she was going to see it through and that's still her motto today. "P" was determined to get her mother and father's attention, they needed to know she was there and wasn't going anywhere! If they were going to take each other down, she was going down with them. Let me tell you, "God is a good God!" Not only did God keep everyone from hurt, harm and danger but "P's" mother and father were together for 56 years until her father went home to be with the Lord on May 23, 2017- *Rest In Eternal Peace Daddy!*

Later on "P" would bring many of her childhood ACEs into her marriage. She didn't realize how much anxiety, anger, stress and un-forgiveness she had on the inside of her. "P" also learned later on in her marriage that she was unable to bear children, which made matters even worse. In spite of "P's" inability to bear children, God blessed her with four beautiful Godchildren whom she loves dearly.

"P" didn't understand that one day God would use her strength and tenacity as His mouthpiece to His people, **"But the Lord said to me, "Do not say, 'I am too young.' You must go to everyone I send you to and say whatever I command you" (Jeremiah 1:7).** How many of you know the devil didn't like the fact that God had a purpose and a plan for "Ps" life **"The thief comes only to steal and kill and destroy, I have come that they may have life, and have it to the full" (John 10:10 NIV)?** No matter what ACEs "P" experienced, they became the foundation of her message of F.A.I.T.H., **"Forsaking All I Trust Him."** God would still get the glory out of every adverse situation and circumstance. **"For I know the plans I have for you declares the Lord, plans to prosper you and not to harm you, plans to give you hope and a future" (Jeremiah 29:11).**

I'd like to tell you a story about "P" when she was fifteen years old.

…. It was a cold Saturday in December 1981, "Ps" mother decided to do something extraordinary, different, unusual - she took all of her children to the mall Christmas shopping which was something absolutely unheard of. She understood very well the hustle and bustle of holiday shopping and the overwhelming crowds they would have to brave, but it was Christmas! "P's" mother laid down the ground rules with all of her children prior to getting out of the car and going into the mall. She said, "I want all of you to stay together so you don't get lost in this craziness!" Do you think they all listened? Not "P", she had her mind set on a specific quest. You see she was a very fashionable and classy kind of girl who enjoyed the finer things in life. She was different, set apart and unique! She was even labeled by family members as being hard to please – and don't forget - spoiled!

Like many young people "P" felt the pressure of trying to keep up with the latest and greatest fashions in school and the neighborhood trends. She actually got her first job at the age of thirteen through the Youth Summer Program where she was introduced to responsibility and earning her own money at a pretty early age. On this particular day she had her mind set on her favorite perfume at Leggett Department store called *"Scoundrel" by Revlon*, "Oh yeah", she said, that stuff was the bomb and you could smell it for miles! At that time it cost about $70 but that didn't matter, she just had to have it. There was only one small

F.A.I.T.H. – Forsaking All I Trust Him

problem. She had spent all of her money on other Christmas items she had purchased. Out of curiosity, she wondered, just how hard would it be to shoplift? She had already witnessed some friends do it for years and they were good at it too, so they thought! You could go in the store with them, pick out all the clothes and shoes you wanted and then leave the store and go back to the car. Before long they would come out loaded with everything you wanted and more! How many of you know those you hang around you become so you know what happened next right? Yep, "P" decided to take the chance of stealing the perfume. Placing the bottle of perfume into the bag with other items she had purchased, she left Leggett's and was nearly out of the mall when she felt a stern tap on her shoulder by a tall Caucasian lady in plain clothes. "Oh My God!" The lady informed "P" that she had reason to believe that she had taken something from the store without paying for it and asked if she would come back with her to the store to answer some questions. "P's" heart began to pound outside of her chest! Have you ever been at a place in your life where you literally thought you got away with something but you really didn't? **"Nothing in all creation is hidden from God's sight. Everything is uncovered and laid bare before the eyes of him to whom we must give account"** (Hebrews 4:13).

By this time, "P" had become very nervous because she knew she was guilty! Her mind began to race, should she run? If she did, would they catch her and if so, would it only make things worse? So many questions raced through her mind. In hope they wouldn't find the perfume she decided to cooperate and follow the lady back to the store. When they arrived the lady called for a police officer and they began interrogating "P" about the merchandise for what seemed like hours but in actuality was only thirty minutes. The police officer gave "P" the option of searching her person or she could surrender the merchandise on her own. "P" finally broke down and surrendered the *"Scoundrel"* perfume.

      Meanwhile her family had finished their shopping and after looking all over the mall for "P" and even having her paged by mall security with no response they returned to their car. Little did they know, "P" had just spent the last hour being interrogated about what would soon become a misdemeanor charge! All she could think of was what would her mother say and, what would her siblings and everyone else who thought so highly of her think? Once the police were finished with the questioning and explaining to "P" what would happen next they told her she could go but they had to release her into a parent's custody because she was a juvenile. "P" informed the officer that she had come to the mall with her family who by this time were probably worried sick and looking all over for her. The officer then escorted "P" out of the mall to the area where she remembered the car being parked. "P" hoped her family had not left her. Fortunately, they were still there. The officer explained the shoplifting charge to "P's" mother, asked her to sign some papers and informed her mother that she would receive additional paperwork in the mail about the court date. Then he released "P" into her mother's custody. The look of disgust and disappointment on everyone's face as she climbed into the back seat of the car was something she will never forget. *Oh the embarrassment and*

F.A.I.T.H. – Forsaking All I Trust Him

shame "P" felt on the inside. She thought her life was ruined for sure.

That was a long ride home for "P!" She prayed silently to herself as she gazed out of the window feeling sick to her stomach! One thing that came to mind on the ride home was not only had she let her family down but also she had let God down. One of the commandments she had learned in Sunday school was, "thou shall not steal," but why hadn't she listened? When the family arrived back home, "P" had dinner then was sent to her room to think about what had happened that day. As she laid there thinking about all that had happened she knew she was going to "get it" more from mom than dad because, after all, she was *"boo and pootie rat"* and could do no wrong in dad's eyes. Later that night "P's" mother placed her on punishment for a couple of weeks which meant no hanging out in Fredericksburg with her cousins or doing any of the fun activities she enjoyed such as Skate Land, house parties and sleepovers with friends. Oh well, it was well deserved. There was one more thing "P" remembered she needed to do and that was to repent (feel or express sincere regret or remorse about one's wrongdoing or sin) and ask God for forgiveness for stealing the perfume. After doing this she cried herself to sleep.

Waking up she wished it were all a dream! What would her legal consequences be? Would she have to spend time in a juvenile center? How would God see her through this painful experience? But see her through He did! In what seemed to be so insurmountable at that time, God's grace and mercy prevailed! "P's" sentence was 80 hours of community service, a suspended driver's license for six months, one year of probation and she was banned from Leggett's Department store until adulthood!

Whew! Surely, God had big plans for her life and had captured her attention for sure because things could have been so much worse! She made a vow to the Lord that day that when she was of age she would pay it forward by volunteering and ministering to those who are incarcerated by sharing her testimony. God's GRACE and MERCY had delivered her and given her another chance to get it right! If you haven't figured it out already, that fifteen-year-old girl named "P" is me! I am humbled and thankful to God for His unfailing love, grace, mercy and forgiveness! Some might say, oh that's nothing compared to what others have gone through but I say, "It's my STORY for God's GLORY!" My question to you is, *"What's Your Story?"*

"Shadrach, Meshach and Abednego came out of the fire, and the satraps, prefects, governors and royal advisers crowded around them. They saw that the fire had not harmed their bodies, nor was a hair of their heads singed; their robes were not scorched, and there was no smell of fire on them" (Daniel 3:27). Not only will God bring you out of the fire as he did Shadrach, Meshach and Abednego but you will come out not smelling like smoke! In other words, there will be no residue of your past for the blood of the lamb has washed it away! **"I even I am he that blots out all of your transgressions and your sins I will remember no more" (Isaiah 43:25).** Jesus declares that not only will He forgive us of our sins but He will remember them no more. He takes no pleasure in holding anything over our heads, that's the trick of the enemy to keep you in condemnation (feeling guilty, ashamed, disapproved)

F.A.I.T.H. – Forsaking All I Trust Him

but God said **"There is therefore now no condemnation to them which are in Christ Jesus, who walk not after the flesh, but after the spirit" (Romans 8:1).**

I was searching for love in all the wrong people, places and things. Although I had accepted the Lord Jesus Christ as my personal Savior, there was still so many times I felt all alone in life! I didn't know just how much my heavenly father loved me and while I may have felt alone, I was really never alone because God was right there with me all the time. I knew about the things of God "Religion" and how to DO church, but I didn't truly have a "Relationship" with God! FEAR (False Evidence Appearing Real) and anxiety had gripped my life and I was wearing a mask to cover up all my hurt, pain, guilt, shame and un-forgiveness. Are you wearing a mask today to cover up your hurt, pain, guilt, shame and un-forgiveness? If so, I encourage you to pray this prayer with me, believe it in your heart and receive God's unconditional love.

….Father God, I come to you today wounded and scarred but I ask you to come into my life and take total control, forgive me of my sins, help me to forgive myself, forgive others and give me a fresh start. I thank you for sending your son Jesus to die on the cross for all of my hurts, pain, guilt and shame and setting me free from all my fears and un-forgiveness. I release the masks and receive your unconditional love in Jesus name, Amen.

REGINA PRICE

INTRODUCTION – FAITH SHIFT

According to Hebrews 11:1, *"Faith* is the substance of things hoped for the evidence of things not seen". During my tenure at World Harvest Bible College in Colum*bus,* Ohio, Holy Spirit revealed this acronym of *"Faith"* to me that prompted me to title this book – **Forsaking All I Trust Him**. Let's take a walk down memory lane with what I call one of many *"Faith Shifts"* in my life. In 1987 I married the man I loved with all my heart. We had met while I was attending National Business College in Roanoke, VA. He was seventeen, I was eighteen and we married three years later. We were young and so in love…

We didn't really know what we were doing and no one gave us an instruction manual on marriage. We had attended a couple of weeks of marriage counseling but other than that we were on our own to figure this thing out and it wasn't easy. Don't get me wrong, those were some best of times but also some worst of times. We separated on several occasions but always seemed to sweep things under the rug enough to get back together again with no real healing from all the hurt and pain that we caused one another. I'm reminded of this story.

"There once was a little boy who had a bad temper. His father gave him a bag of nails and told him that every time he lost his temper, he must hammer a nail into the back of the fence. The first day the boy had driven 37 nails into the fence. Over the next few weeks, as he learned to control his anger, the number of nails hammered daily gradually dwindled down. He discovered it was easier to hold his temper than to drive those nails into the fence. Finally the day came when the boy didn't lose his temper at all. He told his father about it and the father suggested that the boy now pull out one nail for each day that he was able to hold his temper. The days passed and the young boy was finally able to tell his father that all the nails were gone. The father took his son by the hand and led him to the fence He said, 'You have done well, my son, but look at the holes in the fence. The fence will never be the same. When you say things in anger, they leave a scar just like this one. You can put a knife in a man and draw it out. It won't matter how many times you say I'm sorry, the wound is still there.'" The little boy then understood how powerful his words were, He looked up at his father and said, "I hope you can forgive me father for the holes I put in you." "Of course I can," said the father. *(Inspiration Peak, 1997-2008)*

A verbal wound is as bad as a physical one and there were times when my husband and I would use words to wound one another. We didn't have the wisdom of God for our marriage, or know the real meaning of love. **"Love is patient, love is kind. It does not envy, it does not boast, it is not proud. It does not dishonor others it is not self-seeking, it is not easily angered, it keeps no record of wrongs. Love does not delight in evil but rejoices with the truth. It always protects, always trusts, always hopes, always persevere. Love never fails" (1 Corinthians 13:4- 8).** No matter how many times my husband and I eventually said, "I'm sorry", the wounds were still there. Those ACEs had now followed me into my marriage and little did I know but my husband obviously had some of his own ACEs that he was dealing with. I now realize that unhealed people attract unhealthy relationships and hurting people hurt others. Our marriage was falling apart and we had no clue how to fix it! We prayed, sought Biblical counseling from our Pastor but the pride of life and those ACEs overtook us.

We were both serving in ministry, but how many of you know that when God has a purpose and plan for your life the attacks of the devil intensify. Our marriage was under attack and I was dying! Perhaps you are at this very place in your life and you feel there is no hope. God is an ever-present help in the time of trouble and He is able to keep you and deliver you from all of your distresses. **"Seek the LORD while he may be found; call on him while he is near" (Isaiah 55:6).**

It was a holiday Monday, September 5, 2001, and I was on vacation for the entire week. It had been a long sixteen years and I can remember hearing Holy Spirit say, "I want you to spend your entire week of vacation with me." He knew I desperately needed a word for my life and I wasn't letting go until God blessed me and gave me some direction. God had promised Jacob that through him would become great nations but Jacob was a man of many struggles and fears. He had family struggles, a brother Esau who vowed to kill him and a father-in-law who deceived him of his rights to marry his daughter. The struggle with God would be different! Jacob wrestled with the angel of the Lord all night long and said, "I'm not letting you go until you bless me." In the process, Jacob's name was changed to "Israel", May God Prevail!

I too was determined not to let go of God until He blessed me.

F.A.I.T.H. – Forsaking All I Trust Him

In obedience I spent the week praying, fasting and listening to God as He had said. On Wednesday, which was the third day of fasting and praying, I was lying prostrate on my family room floor before God when I undoubtedly heard the spirit of the Lord speak to me just as He had spoken to Abram, **"Leave your country and your relatives and go to the land that I will show you" (Genesis 12:1).** I didn't understand exactly what Holy Spirit was saying at that time until I was able to raise my head up enough from the floor to turn on the T.V. and tune into the Word Network. There was a mandate given to the world by Pastor Rod Parsley, Pastor of World Harvest Church in Columbus, OH to enroll in World Harvest Bible College (WHBC)**"The School of the Spirit".** He stated that "there is someone watching this broadcast right now that has been praying and believing God for a word for your situation! You are sick and tired of being sick and tired and your answer is right here at World Harvest Bible College. You need to get here and get here now! Look straight ahead and select 'Go' and get here as fast as you can."

Instantly, I received this word in my spirit and began to weep uncontrollably because I knew that prophetic word was for me. This was the answer to my prayer even though it made no sense to me at that time but **F.A.I.T.H.** doesn't have to make sense. I quickly said, "Yes Lord I will go" and made a conscientious decision to activate my Faith **"Forsaking All I Trust Him"** to attend Bible College. I knew without a doubt that God had called me to ministry but "What was I called to do and what was my assignment in the earth?" This word from the Lord had nothing to do with my marriage because the one thing I learned is the only person you can change is "YOU!" It had everything to do with the breakthrough God had for me! Now that's a word for someone reading this right now just say, "Yes Lord" to whatever God is calling you to do, **"His mother said to the servants, Do whatever he tells you" (John 2:5)** and God will hasten his word to perform it! It was all still a blur to me, sort of like "P's" experience at age fifteen, and I had so many unanswered questions, "How would God work it all out?"

I immediately began calling the WHBC admissions office to inquire about the process and procedures for enrolling in the school. The instruction given by God concerning this mandate was very clear and concise. He said, "You can't disclose the word received with everyone because not everyone will receive it and the enemy will use others to try and abort what I have spoken to you." As a matter of fact, I couldn't even share it with my husband at that time because as I mentioned earlier, our marriage was falling apart so if God wanted my husband to receive this revelation, He would have to be the one to do it.

Holy Spirit carefully showed me three people God wanted me to share this with to have them pray with me for divine guidance and direction. They each received the news, prayed with me believing if God said it, He would work all things according to His great plan including preparing my husband's heart to receive it and go with me because God does things decently and in order. My faith did not waiver because I had already witnessed the mighty hand of God move in my life as far back as I could remember. He had kept me through some ACEs, allowed me to graduate high school as an honor graduate,

F.A.I.T.H. – Forsaking All I Trust Him

receive a scholarship to attend college in Roanoke, VA, and protected and provided for me along the way. God blessed my husband and I to design and have two homes built, healed my body of tumors, brought me through back surgery and so many more *"Faith Landmarks"* - places of remembrance of His mighty hands carrying me and bringing me through the storms of life.

God was now shifting my faith to a new dimension and preparing me for the place He had predestined for my life. I had to think back on what I already heard and had seen Him do and **"Forsaking All I Trust Him".** The day finally came when the Lord said I could share His plans for my life with my husband as he had already been intercepting phone calls from the Bible College. My husband's response was "That is your thing and I don't want any part of it", so in other words, he wasn't going with me or supporting me. No matter what my husband said, I had to keep focused on the word I received from the Lord. I didn't debate it with him, I just responded "OK" and kept it moving! I was intentional about moving forward with the plans, reminding myself of God's promise to work it out. That's where true faith comes in! Remember, "Faith is the substance of things hoped for, the evidence of things unseen." You don't have to see how it will work out; faith doesn't have to make sense, you just have to believe it and speak it!

Let me tell you how good God is. As I mentioned, I continued to move forward with God's plan to go to WHBC. During this process my husband started intercepting some of the telephone calls I was receiving from them referring to information required to complete my enrollment. I specifically remember one phone call he received informing him that they were still missing a couple of pages of my application and needed me to resubmit it. This made my husband really start to think, *hmmmm*....She is *really serious about this move*. The intercepted phone calls went on for about a month where my husband either heard a message on the answering machine or verbally spoke to someone from the admissions office at WHBC in reference to my application and additional paperwork needed to complete the enrollment process.

What happened next? I'm glad you asked! I was sitting at my desk on a Friday at lunchtime when the telephone rings and guess who it was? You guessed correctly; it was my husband and here's how the conversation went - Husband: "Are you busy?" Me: "I have a few minutes to talk - what's up?" Husband: "I know that I am supposed to go with you." Me: "Oh really, how do you know that you are supposed to go?" Husband: "He told me." Me: "Who is He?" Husband: "God!" It took everything in my power for me not to scream at work but I was so excited that God had given my husband the revelation just like He said he would do! My husband was now willing to complete his part of the application for my acceptance to WHBC. "The Just Shall Live By Faith". You see I didn't get discouraged when my husband said early on that he wasn't going nor did he support my decision to go. What I did was put my trust in the one true God! Just know that if God said it, He will surely bring it to pass.

My husband and I had built a new home about two years prior to this time but that didn't really matter to me as I was willing to leave it all behind in my desperation for a move of God! **"Unless the Lord**

F.A.I.T.H. – Forsaking All I Trust Him

builds a house, the builders labor is in vain" (Psalm 127:1). There was a bunch of chaos and confusion in our home and God is not the author of confusion! Once my husband and I came into agreement about God's plan of relocating to Columbus, Ohio to attend Bible College, we put our home on the market and it sold for more than the asking price in less than two months. "Now that was God!" We gave an advanced notice to our Pastors because we realized how important it was to have the blessing of our spiritual leaders and how you leave one place is how you enter another.

We relocated to the land that God had revealed to me some 500 miles away with no jobs or a place to live by FAITH! When we arrived to Ohio, provision met us there! God had already prepared a suite at a hotel for accommodation with little to no cost per day until we could locate appropriate housing. We knew somebody that knew somebody that knew God and He made a way, Hallelujah! I continued to trust God to order my steps because although my husband was obedient to go where God said to go, his head still had not caught up with his heart. In other words, he still had some doubt in his head how everything would work despite the faith in his heart! Lord I believe; help my unbelief!

We had been in Ohio for three days (**"third day"** means resurrection) when I heard the Spirit of the Lord say, "Rise up Daughter of Zion Today You Will Find Your New Home." I continued to pray for divine guidance and exercised my faith by searching the local housing guides and newspapers for homes in the Reynoldsburg and Pickerington areas to lease since we needed to attain housing pretty quickly. Bible College was starting within the next week so there wasn't much time to waste. I found several homes that I wanted us to go look at and called to make appointments. You will not believe this but the very first home that we drove up to was perfect - God is so good! The home reminded us so much of the one we had just sold in Virginia. It was a Split-Foyer (when you walk in you can go up or down) with an attached garage. Out stepped a tall Caucasian gentleman with blondish colored hair who met us with a firm handshake and a welcoming smile. Mr. Y as we'll call him opened the door and allowed us to take a look at the place and my husband and I both fell in love with the warmth and coziness of the home. My husband informed Mr. Y our purpose for relocating to Ohio was to attend World Harvest Bible College. The landlord was so encouraged by our testimony that he waived the credit and reference checks! Wow, what a confirmation that Holy Spirit was leading and guiding us and things were working together for our good just like we believed and God said He would do!

That's not all we had to exercise faith for. Remember, we had acted on faith and resigned from our jobs prior to our move so what shall we do now? No worries! After watching the hand of God move that quickly with our housing, we were excited to see what His next move would be. We continued to trust that God would do exceedingly abundantly above what we could dare to ask, think or imagine. My husband was an employee for Coca-Cola prior to moving to Ohio and had inquired about receiving a lateral transfer to Coca-Cola in Ohio but things didn't go as planned. As a store merchandiser for Coca-Cola in Fredericksburg he worked manual labor delivering, stocking sodas and building displays at various grocery chains but God had something bigger and better in mind. My husband was offered a position with Pepsi Cola in Ohio and assumed the duties and responsibilities of sitting behind a desk, answering the telephone, processing orders, handling paperwork and creating schedules for other employees – no more manual labor. I'm talking about a man who had minimal office training and computer skills at that time – But God did it!

The Dean of WHBC gave a mandate for all Bible College students to get involved through volunteering in areas of ministry at the school or church and since I had been youth minister at my home church back in Virginia and had a heart toward the youth, I decided to put in a request to volunteer with the Harvest Preparatory School (HPS). Harvest Prep is, a private Christian School for grades K -12. God opened doors for me to volunteer with the Upper School Guidance Counselor and during this time He also granted me favor in the eyes of the Principal who later offered me a full-time job as Administrative Assistant to the Upper School Principal. So now I am not only a Bible College student but also an employee for Harvest Preparatory School. You don't have to make room for your gifts your gifts will make room for you! I can still remember jumping, shouting, praising and thanking God as if I had lost my natural mind – saying, "Look what the Lord has done!" God was faithful, kept His promises, enlarged our territory and blessed us indeed.

While attending Bible classes part-time and working full-time at HPS, I faithfully served in other areas of the ministry such as teaching Heart-to-Heart classes for young girls, assisting with church services in the Jail/Prison as well as the street-witnessing ministry. Four years later I graduated with a degree in Pastoral and General Church Leadership. You see, the School of the Spirit is where I received my total restoration and healing from un-forgiveness. I learned how to forgive myself and others who had hurt me during what I call my *"Silent Years"*. I continue to spread God's love and share my story to the downtrodden and brokenhearted in the jails, street corners and wherever God leads me. My prayer is every word of this book ministers to you and helps to set you *"Free"* as it has done for me. I pray the gift of "Faith" will arise in you. May your spirit man leap with encouragement and expectation to reclaim your destiny and do whatever Holy Spirit leads you to do. **"When Elizabeth heard Mary's greeting, the baby leaped in her womb, and Elizabeth was filled with the Holy Spirit" (Luke 1:41).** Trust God for his divine direction, protection and provision for your life. **It's one thing to talk FAITH it's another thing to live by FAITH!**

F.A.I.T.H. – Forsaking All I Trust Him
CHAPTER 1 – FORSAKING

When you are **"Forsaking"** something you abandon it; quit or leave entirely and become deserted. Abram heard the voice of God call from the deep to leave his place of familiarity and the comfort of family and friends. **"The Lord had said to Abram, 'Go from your country, your people and your father's household to the land I will show you."** God wasn't trying to take something *from* Abram He was actually trying to get something *to* him. God said, **"I will make you into a great nation, and I will bless you. I will make your name great, and you will be a blessing. I will bless those who bless you and whoever curses you I will curse; and all people on earth will be blessed through you" (Genesis 12:1-3).**

God gave Abram a promise that if he is obedient to do what He tells him to do, not only would He bless him, but others would reap the benefit as well. You can only imagine the emotions involved as Abram tried to comprehend it all. There was no itinerary or roadmap that carefully outlined all the details of Abram's journey. Abram couldn't see where he was going nor how he would get there but he chose to walk by faith and not by sight! **"Forsaking"** causes the abandonment of something or someone without hesitation or reservation.

Some scholars believe that Abram disobeyed God's instructions to **"Forsaken"** his family. Abram decided to bring his nephew Lot, the son of his deceased brother Haran on the journey. Listen! **"Obedience is better than sacrifice" (1 Samuel 15:22),** this means, God wants your *obedience*, not your *better idea* so when you decide to bring nephew Tommy along when God specifically says leave him behind there are some consequences to face that could have been avoided. Abram and Lot had to separate on the journey, and it wasn't until they separated that God spoke these words to Abram. **"And the Lord said unto Abram, after Lot was separated from him, Lift up now your eyes, and look from the place where you are northward, and southward, and eastward, and westward. All the land that you see I will give to you and your offspring forever" (Genesis 13:14-15).**

    I wish I could tell you things were easy for Abram after this declaration. If you have read the book of Genesis you know they were not. Abram and his armies had to pursue and then go into battle to rescue his nephew Lot who had pitched his tent at Sodom and Gomorrah, a city of wickedness and depravity, after his separation from Abram. Sodom's sin was so grave that God vowed to destroy the entire city, including Lot and his family. Abram interceded on behalf of the righteous living in Sodom and God promised to spare it if Abram could find at least ten righteous people living in the city. Abram was unsuccessful with his search and while Lot and his family were fleeing Sodom and Gomorrah they were warned by the Angels of God not to look back. Lot's wife disobeyed, looked back, and was turned into a pillar of salt. Lot was saved but what a journey Abram had to endure. There is a price to pay for "Forsaking" – but oh, the reward.

    I realized that in order for me to complete this manuscript I would first need the help of Holy Spirit. Jesus said He would send the Spirit to us to be our Helper, Comforter, and Guide. **"And I will ask the Father, and he will give you another Counselor to be with you**

F.A.I.T.H. – Forsaking All I Trust Him

forever" (John 14:16). Holy Spirit is the one who would ignite my faith! This journey would necessitate some discipline and the **"Forsaking"** of people, places and things. The task would require an escape to a solitary place, one of loneliness and isolation - just as Jesus did when he went into the Garden of Gethsemane to pray. This was no unfamiliar territory for me as I can remember well the many nights of separation from family and friends to complete the required curricula assignments for each of my educational achievements. Once I learned how to deny myself by walking in the spirit instead of catering to what my flesh wanted, what I imagined to be so difficult actually worked together for my good.

So it is with you my friends, when you are obedient in **"Forsaking"** others to fulfill your destiny and purpose in life you must know there is pain before pleasure. One of your biggest deceptions is to believe that everyone will understand and accept your vision, destiny and purpose. Just remember what God has for you is for you and not everyone has your best interest at heart, not even family and friends. You may find yourself in a lonely place which is a good place to be when God is separating you to a desolate place for greatness, not only will you be blessed but others will be blessed through you.

When God gives you a specific direction in **"Forsaking"** something or someone He has purpose in mind. Jesus cried out, **"My God My God why have you Forsaken me?" (Matthew 27:46).** Jesus must have felt that God had completely abandoned him but in actuality God had a purpose and plan for the salvation of all mankind through Jesus' death on the cross. When you make decisions based upon your own intentions, whether good or bad, it is important to consider the impact that it will have on others - Jesus said, **"Not my will Lord but Thy will be done."** Just think if Jesus had not been obedient to the will of his Father there would be no remission of sins and life for the Christian would be meaningless.

Although Abram decided to bring Lot on the journey God still blessed him, changed his name to Abraham and made him the father of nations just as He had declared. Remember in **"Forsaking"** you simply give up something - Webster defines it as such is the way of life, for something better or more appropriate. This was God's will for his son Jesus, His will for Abram, and His will for His sons and daughters. Are you ready to start **"Forsaking"** and walk into your blessings?

F.A.I.T.H. – Forsaking All I Trust Him

"Forsaking" Thoughts/Applications

CHAPTER 2 – ALL

All You Need Is Faith in God! **"I say unto you, That whosoever shall say to this mountain, Be removed, and be cast into the sea; and do not doubt in his heart, but believe that those things which he say shall come to pass, he shall have all he say" (Mark 11:23, Paraphrased).** The word **all** expresses the whole entire quantity or extent of something. **All** consists of everything and there is nothing left because that's **all** there is. Jesus clearly states that **all** you need is faith and your belief in God and whatever mountain stands in your way, you can eradicate it. God gave His **all** when He sacrificed His only begotten Son, Jesus to die on the cross for our sins. Jesus in turn paid it **all** through his shed blood at the cross for **all** mankind.

The songwriter says, "I Surrender **All!**" **All** to Jesus I surrender - **All** to him I freely give…this means you can cast **all** of your cares upon Him because He cares for you. You give **all things up** and over to Jesus. You lay down your life for the sake of Christ and the Gospel. **"For whoever wants to save his life will lose it, but whoever loses his life for me will save it" (Luke 9:24).** When you do this God is pleased and you are adopted into the royal family of Jesus Christ, the One who has called you out of darkness into His marvelous light. His promise to **all** His children is **"You don't have to worry about your life, what you will eat or drink or about your body, what you will wear. If God can feed the birds of the air that do not store up in barns how much more will he do for His children" (Matthew 6:25-26 Paraphrased).** Now that's the secret to **F.A.I.T.H.**

F.A.I.T.H. – Forsaking All I Trust Him

Your heavenly father is omnipotent – **all** powerful, He is omniscient - **all** knowing, and He is omnipresent - **all** over the place at the same time. Therefore, He knows **all** about where you are in your life right now and what you need when you need it. When you put your **F.A.I.T.H.** and trust in the one true God, who made heaven and earth, and don't doubt in your heart, it propels God to honor whatever you ask. God is seeking sons and daughters, children of the Most High God who will believe that **"He is able to do exceedingly abundantly above all that you can ask or think according to the power that works on the inside of you" (Ephesians 3:20 KJV).** Therefore, you can't even begin to see or know **all** that God has prepared for you it has yet to be revealed. You must spend time in prayer, studying His word and put **all** your **F.A.I.T.H.** and trust in Him.

The world and its entire splendor, however, paint's a pretty picture of **all** the things it has to offer. The Bible tells a story in Matthew 4 where Jesus was led by the Spirit into the wilderness to be tempted by the devil with three different "propositions." The third temptation had the devil and Jesus up on a high mountain where **all** the kingdoms of the world and their glory were visible. Satan said to Jesus, **"All this I will give you if you bow down and worship me" (Matthew 4:9).** What baffled me is how Satan believed he could give Jesus something that never belonged to him in the first place. Satan may be the god of this world but **"In the beginning, God created the heavens and the earth" (Genesis 1:1).** Therefore, **all** things were created by God and He has given his children dominion and authority in the earth. Jesus did not succumb to **all** Satan's temptations even in His weakest moments. **"Then Jesus said to him, away from me, Satan!"** For it is written: 'Worship the Lord your God, and serve him only' (Matthew 4:10-11).

"And he said to me, my grace is sufficient for you: for my strength is made perfect in weakness (2 Corinthians 12:9)." When you decide to follow Jesus, temptations will come but He always provides a way of escape for you, **"No temptation has overtaken you except what is common to mankind. And God is faithful he will not let you be tempted beyond what you can bear. But when you are tempted, he will also provide a way out so that you can endure it" (1 Corinthians 10:13)** and **all** His promises for you are yes and Amen, which means So Be It!

Later on in the book of Matthew Peter questioned Jesus. "We have left everything to follow you! What then will be for us?" One might believe that Peter was feeling **all** his labor in following the Lord was in vain, after all, he was *Forsaking* **all** that he had, including his family and friends, to follow the Lord Jesus Christ with much zeal and affection. But what was in it for him in the long run? Peter was thinking about his promotion and advancement of success here on earth. Do you sometimes feel like God has forgotten about you too? Where is your reward on earth for *Forsaking* **all** to follow Christ? Jesus said to them, **"I tell you the truth, at the renewal of all things, when the Son of Man sits on his glorious throne, you who have followed me will also sit on twelve thrones, judging the twelve tribes of Israel" (Matthew 19:27-28).**

Jesus has something far greater in mind for us **all.** He prom-

F.A.I.T.H. – Forsaking All I Trust Him

ises that when the Son of man shall sit on the throne of his glory, He will make **all** things new, and they shall sit with him in judgment of those who will be judged according for their doctrine and beliefs. This sets forth the honor, dignity, and authority of your ministry. Jesus proclaims that everyone who commits to *Forsaking* **all** for the sake of the gospel will receive his compensation and rewards in heaven at last. May you rest your **F.A.I.T.H.** and hope on this promise; then you shall be ready for every service or sacrifice while here on earth with blessed assurance that your heavenly inheritance is not given as earthly ones are, but according to God's good pleasure.

REGINA PRICE

"All" Thoughts/Applications

F.A.I.T.H. – Forsaking All I Trust Him

CHAPTER 3 – I

I asked myself, "Can anything good come out of a small country town called Woodford, Virginia?" Absolutely! So **I** encouraged myself in the Lord just as David did… **And David was greatly distressed; for the people spake of stoning him, because the soul of all the people was grieved, every man for his sons and for his daughters: but David encouraged himself in the Lord his God"** **(1 Samuel 30:8). I** remembered Nathaniel asked that same question about the town of Nazareth, **"Nazareth! Can anything good come from there" (John 1:46)?** Well, something and someone good did come from Nazareth, a carpenter's Son - the Greek word is *Teckton*, which means "builder." Who would have thought a builder would be the atoning sacrifice for the sins of all mankind? Jesus is the ultimate example of *if I can do it surely you can!* He taught us that it doesn't matter where you come from but where you are going. **"For I know the plans I have for you," declares the Lord, "plan's to prosper you, plans to give you hope and a future" (Jeremiah 29:11).**

A word of encouragement to you who are struggling with stepping out in **F.A.I.T.H.,** You can be all that God has created you to be and do all that He has created you to do if you just believe. **F.A.I.T.H.** is action. "Doing" is what you must remember whenever you set your mind to something. The devil will always try to discredit you and make you feel unequipped for the task and count you out but God has counted you in. **I** felt unequipped to write this book but my faith outweighed my fear. **I** had to get out of my feelings and into my spirit, take authority, put one foot in front of another, square my shoulders and remember a famous quote from R.J. Smith, "Nothing beats a failure but a try." I literally put my faith in action to write this manuscript and although every word is written by me, they are inspired by Holy Spirit with hopes that you my friends will be encouraged and empowered to pursue the assignment and promises God has for you also.

I know you may be saying "That's easier said than done" but here's what I say to that, "GET OUT YOUR MIND" so you can "PUT ON THE MIND OF CHRIST" because the battle begins in your mind! You must make things happen instead of sitting back and allowing things to happen. If I can trust Him to do it so can you! I used to sit and meditate on 1 Corinthians 12 concerning "Spiritual Gifts" to see which of those I had been given through the Spirit for the common good. God showed me early on in life that He had not only given me a measure of *saving faith* which all men are given, **"For I say, through the grace given unto me, to every man that is among you, not to think of himself more highly than he ought to think; but to think soberly, according as God hath given to every man the measure of faith" (Romans 12:3)** but the *spiritual gift of faith*. The *spiritual gift* of faith is not to be confused with saving faith. All Christians have been given saving faith (Ephesians 2:8-9), but not all receive this special gift of faith. The word for faith in the New Testament is *Pistis*. It carries the notion of confidence, certainty, trust, and assurance in the object of faith. The gift of faith is rooted in one's saving faith in Christ and the trust that comes through a close relationship with the Savior. Those with this gift have a trust and confidence

F.A.I.T.H. – Forsaking All I Trust Him

in God that allows them to live boldly for Him and manifest that faith in mighty ways. For those who are interested, you can take a survey at *SpiritualGiftsTest.com* to discover your spiritual gifts.

While I couldn't quite grasp this at the time I could remember the bulldog tenacity I had growing up. You see, a bulldog has a tough and tenacious character, a droopy upper lip and his lower jaw is undershot, meaning that his lower teeth stick out farther than his top teeth. The Bulldog's jaws are massive and strong, intended for latching on to his opponent and holding on. Despite cartoon depictions of them as ferocious dogs, today's Bulldogs are bred to be affectionate and kind. They are, indeed, resolute and courageous, but they aren't out to pick a fight. They often have a calm dignity about them when they are mature, and while they are friendly and playful, they can be a bit stubborn and protective of their families. Bulldogs love people. They seek people out for attention and enjoy nothing more than languishing next to their masters, and perhaps snoring while sleeping with their heads in their laps.

This reminds me of the traumatic experience I had with bullying in the sixth grade, unwanted aggressive behavior among school aged children that involves a real or perceived power imbalance. It was one of the worst years of my life! The bulldog tenacity I possessed to get up every morning, in the face of adversity, was absolutely remarkable. I was taught how to read, write and create sentences in school, but no one taught me about bullying. The National Voices for Equality, Education and Enlightenment (NVEEE), statistics show that suicide remains among the leading cause of death, in children, who experience bullying (usually by hanging), 15% of school absenteeism is directly related to fears of being bullied at school and 56% of students have personally witnessed some type of bullying at school.

What I realized was every adverse situation that I faced in life prepared me for what is now my purpose, to save lives! Joseph said to his brothers, **"And now, do not be distressed and do not be angry with yourselves for selling me here, because it was to save lives that God sent me ahead of you." (Genesis 45:5).** **"You intended to harm me, but God intended it for good to accomplish what is now being done, the saving of many lives." (Genesis 50:20).** As an adult, I have had the opportunity to become a substitute teacher and educate many children about the negative effects of bullying.

I have worked with youth in some capacity or another most of my life. I guess it was God's way of showing me that although I was unable to conceive children of my own that He would bless me with countless children. I can recall attending a "Youth First" conference that builds' stronger communities by promoting collaboration amongst youth serving agencies. The keynote speaker, an expert on personal development and human potential presented everyone with the question, "What-If?" This presentation inspired every youth worker to look at problems and impossibilities and instead of turning away, ask, **"What if we could? I know we can't, but what if WE could?"** Thinking like this would cause us to set inspirational goals, perform like experts, and achieve transformational results. The presentation wasn't just about what the speaker had seen or heard but how he considered and applied this same question, "What-If" to his life of success. He used

F.A.I.T.H. – Forsaking All I Trust Him

his amazing guitar work and comedy to inspire and re-energize those in attendance to make real change. He said to survive and thrive today you must **embrace and create change**, step out and define the curve rather than follow it. But here's the thing... the very innovation and change you need is right there inside you, in your unique abilities and experiences. You are already equipped with the exact tools you need to tap into your bountiful well of ideas, performance and abundance.

So, "What-if" you tried to do the one thing that you feared to do for so long? What's the worst thing that could happen? Two things, either it doesn't turn out the way you hoped for and, if it doesn't, you can try again or "What-if" it did turn out the way you hoped for? How would you know the outcome if you never put forth the effort? I will say this again, "The only obstacle standing in your way is "you." Don't live a life of "what-ifs" and "regrets", it's high time for you to step out in **F.A.I.T.H. now!**

Here's what **I** told myself. This book may not be for **everyone** but it is surely for **someone**. The Lord answered Habakkuk and said, **"Write the vision and make it plain so those who read it will run with it" (Habakkuk 2:2 paraphrased).** I realize that some of you who are reading this book at this very moment are prolific writers, best-selling authors and publishers of numerous books. However, I'm sure there was a starting point full of doubts, what-ifs and I cant's but you turned your doubt into do, your what-if into why not and your "**I can't**" into "**I can!**"

REGINA PRICE

"I" Thoughts/Applications

F.A.I.T.H. – Forsaking All I Trust Him

CHAPTER 4 – TRUST

As I mentioned earlier in the book, Holy Spirit is good at giving me acronyms for words. **TRUST - Totally Rely Upon Someone or Something Trustworthy.** A simple definition of **TRUST**, according to Merriam-Webster, is belief that someone or something is reliable, good, honest and effective. So it is safe to say that when you trust someone or something you don't have to fear. When Holy Spirit prompted me to write this book, He said you have two choices, you can respond with **FEAR – False Evidence That Appears Real** and reject what I called you to do or you can walk by **F.A.I.T.H. – Forsaking All I Trust Him** and accept what I called you to do!

My Pastor, Fred Wyatt has the anointed gift of teaching the word of God! When teaching a sermon series called, "Winning the Mind" He said, "The quality of life is predicated upon your mind!" If you have not renewed your mind for the promises of God then you can be walking around as a saved Christian but not living the quality of life God has for you. Fear is the one thing that rejects the promise and causes you to take an alternative route and fail to **Trust** God!" Fear keeps you living at the status quo and in a place of comfort and familiarity. Fear stagnates your **F.A.I.T.H.** and leads you to believe that you have to be totally equipped, have it all together or be the perfect Christian to walk out the promises of God instead of **Trusting** Him to equip you, teach you and mature you along the way. All God wants is a "Yes!" Can you say "YES LORD?"

It wasn't until I stopped fighting to write this book called, "*For-*

saking All I **Trust** *Him"* and started *doing* it all the things I had **trusted** God for, such as becoming an author, self-publisher and reaching people all over the world, began to come to pass! **"Some trust in chariots and some in horses, but we trust in the name of the LORD our God" (Psalm 20:7).** Here's what David knew about the situation; when he went to war against his enemies; despite all the great strength of their horses and chariots that give support to winning a battle he would not fear because his VICTORY rested with the Lord! Who or what do you put your **trust** in?

Is your **trust** in something as effortless as believing your car will start each morning when you get in it for work? Perhaps you **trust** that the pilot is well trained and equipped to navigate the plane in order to get you safely from one destination to another. If so, your mind is telling you that it is okay to **trust** without putting a great deal of thought to it. Could it be that if you can put your **trust** in something or someone so unreliable and unknown then you have enough faith to **trust** God for your BIGGEST DREAM? I want to encourage you today to "DREAM BIG!" The very thing that you think is so impossible or foolish is the very thing that God wants to use to shame the wise. **"Instead, God chose things the world considers foolish in order to shame those who think they are wise. And he chose things that are powerless to shame those who are powerful" (1 Corinthians 1:27, NLT).** I promise you that whatever it is that God has called you to IS more afraid of you than you are of IT! The devil is afraid that he will lose and you are going to win every time! Say this with me, **"I must learn to Totally Rely Upon God who is Trustworthy in every**

F.A.I.T.H. – Forsaking All I Trust Him

situation and circumstance in my life because I am Winning!"

I had to totally **Trust** God for his divine presence, protection, provision and promise for my life when I answered the call to leave my place of familiarity and relocate to Columbus, OH. I can assure you that the moment I decided to "GET OUT OF MY MIND" long enough to HEAR IN MY SPIRIT and make the conscientious decision to trust and obey it literally changed the course of my life forever and has taken me to a place of no return. I can no longer settle for the mundane and mediocre, I **Trust** God for the extraordinary! Being compelled to write this book came as no surprise to me but it doesn't mean my **F.A.I.T.H.** has not been tested. I had to put my **F.A.I.T.H.** in action and win the battle against my mind. I remember when Holy Spirit finally revealed this to me sitting at the aforementioned "Release the Chains" Life Class Experience for Women. I learned the Seven Strategies to Releasing the Chains. 1) You have to accept the fact that you will have to stretch, and build your muscles but the pain will be worth it, 2) Get honest with the truth of who you are and the value that you provide to other people, 3) Assign value to your failures instead of fearing them, 4) Reduce the number of steps that it takes to reach your goal, instead of 10,000 steps take 50 steps, 5) Decide that intimidation is for suckers, people are people and you don't need someone else's approval, 6) Surround yourself with people who are playing much bigger than you and making things happen 7) Invest in "Yourself" even when it seems scary and you don't have enough!

These strategies grabbed my attention and got my adrenaline going! I had to tell myself, "Regina you can do it" and "With God All

Things Are Possible!" Satan is very cunning and he is always looking for a way to distract you. I can't even tell you all the types of distractions to come my way since starting to write this manuscript but I set a goal for myself to complete this book and if you are reading it, God's plan prevailed!

That's what I recommend for you whenever God gives you an assignment, you must set goals and make up in your mind that not only are you going to say "YES LORD" but also you are going to be a finisher! Finisher's set goals, plan, strategize and never quit; they run their race with grace, courage and anticipation knowing that if they keep to the course sooner or later they will win the prize! The Apostle Paul was an excellent example of being motivated to finish. In fact, he was so motivated that he challenged the Corinthian church that in whatever they do to press on to the finish line and win the prize! Oh what joy must have filled Paul's heart to know that at the end of his life he had **"Fought a Good Fight, Finished the Race and Kept the Faith" (2 Timothy 4:7 NIV)!**

F.A.I.T.H. – Forsaking All I Trust Him
"Trust" Thoughts/Applications

CHAPTER 5 – HIM

The word **HIM** defined by Webster is used as the object of a verb or preposition to refer to a male person or animal previously mentioned or easily identified. Thus far we have discussed **Forsaking, All, I, Trust** and the last chapter of this book I would like to focus on the **HIM** that makes it all possible! I refer to **HIM** as King of Kings, Lord of Lords - The Great I Am That I Am! This **HIM** is Jehovah Jireh, - "My Provider", Jehovah Rophe, - "My Healer", Jehovah Nissi, - "My Banner of Protection", Jehovah Shalom, -"My Peace"! He is bread when I am hungry, water when I am thirsty, **"I was young and now I am old, yet I have never seen the righteous Forsaken nor his children begging bread" (Psalms 37:25 NIV)**! The **HIM** I am talking about is no other than my Master, Savior, Abba Father and Friend. His name is **Jesus, Y'shua!**

I could not have written this book without **HIM** and the guidance of His precious Holy Spirit **"But the Advocate, the Holy Spirit, whom the Father will send in my name, will teach you all things and will remind you of everything I have said to you" (John 14:26 NIV)**. I encourage you to allow God to catapult your **F.A.I.T.H.** to a new dimension and Holy Spirit to give you what to say, how to say it and when to say it for the assignment God has called you to. **"Be strong and courageous. Do not be afraid or terrified because of them, for the Lord your God goes with you; he will never leave you nor forsake you" (Deuteronomy 31:6 NLT)**. In **HIM** rests His promise that He will go before you and make every crooked path straight, He will be with you until the end of the world and He will even make your enemies be at peace with you. They will not refute or criticize the work of your hands that God has formed and fashioned for His glory! I urge you today to take charge of reclaiming your destiny as I have faithfully done! "I am Free Praise the Lord, I'm Free!" The Chains Have Been Released!

"In HIM also, when you heard the word of truth, the gospel of your salvation, and believed in HIM, were sealed with the promised Holy Spirit" (Ephesians 1:13 ESV). We have heard the word and believed unto salvation in a God whom we have not seen yet we believe exists because Holy Spirit, Spirit of Truth, has revealed and sealed this truth about God in our hearts through His written and preached word. If you can believe in a God whom you have not seen, that He loved you so much to honor His plan of salvation for all humankind by delivering over His only begotten son, Jesus, to die on the cross for the atonement of all sin surely you can trust that He loves you enough to see you through His plan and purpose for your life. You might ask, what are His plans and His purpose for my life? **"And you will seek Me and find Me, when you search for Me with all your heart" (Jeremiah 29:13 NKJV).** This means pulling your heart back from the things of the world, giving it to the Lord and spending quality time with **HIM** in prayer!

Prayer can open doors to what a finite human mind can **only** comprehend from an infinite Holy God! Jeremiah was urged to pray on behalf of the people and God promised to answer him and reveal the plans He had for them, **"Call to Me and I will answer you, and**

I will tell you great and mighty things, which you do not know" (Jeremiah 33:3 NASB). After all, who is a better person to ask about His purpose and plan than the one who created you? **"For in him all things were created: things in heaven and on earth, visible and invisible, whether thrones or powers or rulers or authorities; all things have been created through him and for him" (Colossians 1:16 NIV).** When you purchase appliances and there is a question about the operation, you consult the manufacturer or seller of the product who can best answer your question. God your creator desires you to consult **HIM** so He can reveal to you great and mighty things you do not know. He wants to start pouring out His heart to you once you give your heart to **HIM!** You must be willing to humble yourself, focus your ear to hear and your heart to receive and let **HIM** order your steps **"A man's mind plans his way [as he journeys through life], But the Lord directs his steps and establishes them" (Proverbs 16:9 AMP).**

Jesus took Peter, James and John with **HIM** into the Garden of Gethsemane to watch for **HIM** while He prayed to the Father about the task that was at hand. Jesus did not want to suffer but He knew He would have to suffer for the sins of all mankind and chose to obey, **"Father, if you are willing, take this cup from me; yet not my will, but yours be done." (Luke 22:42 NIV).** If Jesus can humbly and actively submit **Himself** to death on the cross so we can live forever in eternity, then we too must be willing to go through some stretching, suffering with perseverance, persistence, and pursuit of fulfilling God's ultimate plan and purpose for your life through **F.A.I.T.H.!** It's time

F.A.I.T.H. – Forsaking All I Trust Him

to step out of the boat. **"Come", he said. Then Peter got down out of the boat, walked on the water and came toward Jesus (Matthew 14:29).** Peter walked upon the water by his **F.A.I.T.H.** and the power of Jesus Christ. Surely, if Peter and I can step out of the boat and overcome the fear of the water, anxiety, struggles and disappointments of life to get to *"Destiny"* in **HIM** so can you! Then! **"Rejoice always and delight in your F.A.I.T.H.; be unceasing and persistent in prayer; in every situation (no matter what the circumstances) be thankful and continually give thanks to God; for this is the will of God for you in Christ Jesus. (1 Thessalonians 5:16-18 AMP)!**

REGINA PRICE
"Him" Thoughts/Applications

F.A.I.T.H. – Forsaking All I Trust Him
CONCLUSION

I once preached a message called, "What Is Faith?" Some may think of faith as a supernatural force. Some say if you have enough faith you'll get rich, stay healthy and live a contented life but how does one have enough faith? Others might say that faith is when you put your trust, confidence, assurance or belief in something and these all are true but according to the Apostle Paul, there is more to faith than just believing. "Faith is also a Spirit." **It is written: "I believed; therefore, I have spoken." Since we have that same spirit of faith, we also believe and therefore speak (2 Corinthians 4:13).** So then faith is believing and speaking.

It is not good enough for you to just believe in something but you must speak it into existence. **"Death and life are in power of the tongue and those who love it will eat its fruit" (Proverbs 18:21).** Caleb and Joshua were the only first generation Israelites to make it into the Promised Land because not only did they believe that they could go up, overtake and possess the land but they spoke it with authority, power and the same Spirit of Faith! Everyone else was speaking the opposite but they said, **"The land we passed through and explored is exceedingly good. If the Lord is pleased with us, HE will lead us into that land, a land flowing with milk and honey, and will give it to us" (Numbers 14:8).**

Another attribute of Faith is Action! **What good is it, my brothers, if someone says he has faith but does not have works? Can that faith save him? If a brother or sister is poorly clothed** and lacking in daily food, and one of you says to them, "Go in peace, be warmed and filled," without giving them the things needed for the body, what good is that? So also faith by itself, if it does not have works, is dead" (James 2:14-17). You must be willing to put your faith to work. What good is it for a construction worker to have all the necessary tools, skills and understanding of how to build but never apply that which he has been gifted with? There would be no buildings!

I also talked about the three things that define faith and the first was assurance. Based on the amplified version of **Hebrews 11:1, "Now faith is the assurance (title, deed, confirmation) of things hoped for (divinely guaranteed), and the evidence of things not seen (the conviction) of their reality – faith comprehends as fact what cannot be experienced by the physical senses."** One must have assurance - a positive declaration intended to give you confidence. This type of assurance and confidence is compared to the characteristics of a palm tree. A palm tree is a wonderfully diverse species that can grow up to 197 feet tall whether in the desert or a rainforest. Coconuts, dates, betel nuts and acai fruit all come from palm trees. John 12:3 says, **They took palm branches and went out to meet Him shouting, "Hosanna!" Blessed is he who comes in the name of the Israel!"** The palm tree was a sign of joy and victory as they met the King Messiah, who was about to make His public entrance into Jerusalem, in triumph; and where, by His sufferings and death, He should gain the victory over sin. But the most amazing fact about the palm tree is its roots not only spread wide but they also run deep so when strong winds come, the palm tree's root system will bend but not break!

Someone reading this book right now needs to know that you can have assurance and confidence that when you make the decision to embrace and create change in your life whether it is writing a book, getting a college degree, relocating to another area or simply giving up a habit, you will be stretched like a palm tree. However, through this stretching your faith will grow stronger and stronger! Say this with me, "I may Bend but I will not Break!" The second thing that defines faith is "Divinely Guaranteed – proceeding from God: divine laws. So what if God does not remove the thorn in your side, people who don't believe in you or support you? Paul said, **"Three different times I begged the Lord to take it away. Each time he said, My grace is all you need, My power works best in weakness, so now I am glad to boast about my weaknesses, so that the power of Christ can work through me. That's why I take pleasure in my weaknesses, and in the insults, hardships, persecutions, and troubles that I suffer for Christ, For when I am weak, than I am strong" (2 Corinthians 12:8-10).**

Faith says, "Father if you are willing, take this cup from me; yet not my will, but yours be done." Are you willing to die to self, persevere through the hard time and fulfill the task at hand? The final thing that defines your faith is "Evidence of the unseen". In other words faith extends far beyond what your eyes can see, ears can hear or your feet can touch. What is Faith? Faith is simply, knowing and trusting God! It is believing the word you have received, activating your faith through application, putting it to work by doing something and then speaking and calling those things that be not seen at that very moment into existence. A *"fact"* doesn't necessarily mean it is the *"truth!"* It may be a fact that the doctor gives you a bad report, but the truth is, "By His stripes you are healed!" The truth is when you put your faith in action God will perfect that which concerns you, His mercy towards you endures forever and He will not forsake the work of His hands. Selah! That means pause and think about everything I have shared with you and walk it out by F.A.I.T.H. Amen!

Sincerely,
Regina Price

F.A.I.T.H. – Forsaking All I Trust Him

SALVATION PRAYER

Father God, I come to you today realizing I am a sinner in need of a Savior. I repent of my sins and ask you Lord Jesus to forgive me of my sins and come into my life and into my heart. I confess with my mouth and believe in my heart that Jesus died on the cross for my sins, He was buried and that God raised HIM from the dead on the third day and my sins have been forgiven. I receive you now Lord Jesus as my Savior and my Lord and I ask you to take complete control of my life and use it to glorify your kingdom here on earth. From this day forward I will live for you as you show me how. Thank you Lord Jesus for forgiving me, saving me and cleansing me with your precious blood! In Jesus name I pray, Amen! If you prayed this simple prayer, I encourage you to get connected to a Bible believing and word teaching church, where you can learn and grow in the principles of God's word.

REGINA PRICE
F.A.I.T.H. PRAYER

Father God, thank you that I walk by *"Faith"* and not by sight! Therefore, my *"Faith"* is not based upon what I can see; if I can see it then it is temporary and subject to change. I believe that I can have what God says I can have, be who God says I can be and do what God says I can do by *"Faith!"* I bind the spirit of fear and I loose the spirit of *"Faith"* over my mind and over my life. Today, I choose to unleash my *"Faith"* and whatsoever I confess with my mouth and believe in my heart I shall have it and by the confession of my *"Faith"* it shall not fail me. I thank you Father God that it is by *"Faith"* that I have Favor with God and Favor with Man and my *"Faith"* opens doors to supernatural increase. I believe by *"Faith"* that every provision for every purpose and promise God has spoken over my life is already provided and shall come to pass because of my *"Faith!"* Thank you Father God that my *"Faith"* is likened unto a Palm Tree, it is upright and deeply rooted, always looking towards heaven, it flourishes and is not affected by my situations and circumstances, it may bend but not break! In Jesus name I pray, Amen!

F.A.I.T.H. – Forsaking All I Trust Him
UNDERSTANDING AND CONQUERING ACEs

Dear Readers,

As I prepared to go to print with this manuscript I felt like I needed to talk a little bit more about Adverse Childhood Experiences (ACEs) and how those ACEs became the "root cause" of the problems within my marriage and other things I've struggled with in my life. Until you are able to identify the root cause or source of problems or issues it is difficult to resolve or reach a solution. Drugs, alcohol addiction, smoking, uncontrollable rage, pedophilia, etc. are merely symptoms of the root cause of fear, anxiety, domestic violence and molestation.

Through God's grace I have been able to recognize, confront and conquer many of my "root issues". I am by no means a finished work and I still have to allow Him to reveal areas in my life that I need to work on. I think we all need that because what we fail to confront and conquer will one day rise up and confront and conquer us. I hope this Bonus Chapter on Understanding and Conquering ACEs will help you get a better understanding of how our childhood experiences shape our lives in both a positive and negative way and will help you, the reader, recognize, confront and conquer any root issues that may be holding you back from being the best person you can be.

REGINA PRICE

Recognize

The first step in conquering ACEs is to recognize if you are experiencing ACEs. ACEs can be recognized by a person's reoccurring manifestation of uncontrollable outbursts and nonverbal behavior patterns such as depression, anger, anxiety, panic attacks, psychosis, even suicide attempts in childhood years. All or some of these can follow you into your adult life if unrecognized and addressed appropriately. I was a nail bitter for many years due to stress, fear and anxiety. I developed a hiatal hernia at an early age and suffered reproductive issues. I didn't realize just how many symptoms of those ACEs I exemplified until they were manifested in my marriage. I was very controlling and possessed an uncontainable amount of rage toward my husband when I believed he was being manipulative or if he returned home at a much later time than he originally stated he would return. I had some serious trust issues! I was so afraid that he would leave the home and not return for days like "P's" dad that I wanted to know and control where my husband was at all times. The very dysfunction and generational sins that "P" stated she wanted no part of had now followed her into her (my) marriage. My voice would escalate pretty quickly when trying to get my point across and my husband would say, "The first thing you need to do is, 'Tone It Down!'" He wasn't much of the arguing or fighting type; as a matter of fact, he would leave the home again or get the remote, turn the television to his favorite show and increase the volume to tune me out. This escalated my anger and my next reaction was to use verbal and/or physical abuse toward my husband as this was the model of behavior "P" witnessed growing up. I thank God that my husband would leave the home to give me time to calm down or who knows what could have happened.

Perhaps you are a victim of ACEs from experiencing violence in the home, separation and divorce of parents, abandonment, neglect, economic hardship, having an incarcerated parent, watching or being the victim of sexual abuse, living with parents who are alcoholics and drug addicts, having a parent who is depressed or suffering with a mental illness or maybe you've even witnessed a murder. Subconsciously, you now have a severe anger problem which causes you to self-mutilate or abuse others, or maybe alcohol, drugs, food or sex is your coping mechanism. You find yourself yelling, screaming, and physically abusing your children, husband, wife, girlfriend or boyfriend because that's what you experienced. Perhaps, mom and dad left you home alone with a brother, sister, uncle or family friend who molested you and now you are depressed all the time, bedwetting into adulthood, confused about your gender identity or have become an obnoxious pedophile. Your family experienced financial hardship growing up and you are determined that you will never live another day of your life in poverty so you become a drug dealer, use others for money or even lie or steal to get ahead. The question is no longer, "Why did you do it?" but "What happened to you?"

Confront

If you are going to be the person God has called you to be, and fulfill the assignments He has for you to do in the earth by F.A.I.T.H. you must learn how to confront your ACEs. One of the principles I learned as a Restorative Justice Facilitator, is there must be a safe space created in order for the victim, offender and community member to come together and decide how to confront the issues and repair the harm done. Instead of using the blame, shame and punishment routine, journalist, Jane Stevens, discusses the new unified science of human development - understanding and nurturing to get people to a safe space so they can use their thinking brain and not their fight, flight or fright brain, to begin healing themselves. Stevens gave an example of the approach a high school principal in Walla, Walla, Washington used to explore some of the ACEs kids dealt with and how to help them understand and confront them.

The principal trained his staff to move from the traditional "hammer" approach to a more inquisitive one. When there was a student who threw a chair in the classroom or cursed at a teacher, instead of using punishment the teacher would ask the student, "What's going on?" or "What happened to you?" The child would eventually break down, start crying and say, "My dad's an alcoholic and he beat up my mom last night. The police came and took my dad to jail, my mom went to the hospital and I had to take care of my brother and sister." As a result of identifying what happened to the child, the teachers are now able to address the *root cause* of the anger - which is domestic violence - and respond to the trauma appropriately. Within three years of putting this approach into practice, the student's suspension rate dropped 90% and administrators stopped expelling students. Test scores, grades, graduation rates and the number of students applying to college increased (*GrassRootsChange, 2015*).

Confrontation is not always easy but it is necessary! To confront something or someone means to evaluate your thoughts and feelings about the situation and how you will respond. Once you have identified the *root cause* of your ACEs, it is important to confront them. This however, does not mean that you need to confront the person(s) that caused you harm face-to-face. While it is beneficial for some people, others may not get the remorse or request for forgiveness they need or desire. The person may not realize or admit to the harm or how it has affected your life. Remember, sin is passed down upon your children's children to the third and fourth generations and the person who caused you the harm was most likely a victim of ACEs themselves.

I'd like to share some practical tools for how I was able to confront the spirit of un-forgiveness. I was watching In Touch Ministries with Dr. Charles Stanley, Pastor of the First Baptist Church in Atlanta, GA. Dr. Stanley was teaching a message on forgiveness. He said forgiveness is for you, not your adversary! You must choose to forgive just as Christ has forgiven you. Forgiveness releases you from the control your adversary has over your mind. Un-forgiveness keeps you in bondage of moving forward and causes severe health issues while the adversary has gone on with their life. I knew in my heart that there were some people in my life that I needed to forgive. I made a conscientious decision to confront those ACEs and complete the steps I learned from Dr. Charles Stanley. I was set free once and for all from un-forgiveness! If you are harboring un-forgiveness in your heart, I pray that putting these steps in action by F.A.I.T.H. will also help you to forgive others and release you from hurt.

• Step 1 - Ask Holy Spirit to help you make a list of all the people you need to forgive and the events you need to forgive them for.

• Step 2 - Arrange two chairs facing each other and seat yourself in one of the chairs.

• Step 3 - Imagine each person on your list is sitting in the other chair. Share everything that you can remember the person has done to hurt you. Do not hold the tears or the emotions that accompany the confessions.

• Step 4 - Choose to forgive the person once and for all and do not doubt what you have said and done is not real and valid.

• Step 5 - Release the person from the apology you feel is owed you for the offense. Say, "You are free and forgiven!"

• Step 6 - If the person is still a part of your life, such as a family member, accept them without wanting to change the aspects of his or her personality or behavior.

• Step 7 - Thank God for using each person as a tool in your life to deepen your insight of His grace and draw you closer to the image of His Son.

• Step 8 - Pray this prayer. Because I am forgiven and accepted by Jesus Christ, I can now forgive and accept you (name each person). I choose now to forgive you no matter what you did to me. I release you from the hurt (name the hurts), and you are no longer accountable to me for them. You are free.

• Step 9 - When you have finished praying through the hurts you have suffered, pray this prayer of faith. Lord Jesus, by faith, I receive Your unconditional love and acceptance in the place of this hurt, and I trust You to meet all my needs. I take authority over the enemy, and in the name of Jesus, I take back the ground I have allowed Satan to gain in my life because of my attitude toward (name the people). Right now, I give this ground back to the Lord Jesus Christ to whom it rightfully belongs, Amen. (*Adapted From, "The Gift of Forgiveness" 1991*)

Conquer

You have recognized, confronted and now it is time to totally conquer those ACEs. While I have referenced several quotes and materials from renowned authors and speakers throughout this book, the most important person who I know that can help you conquer those ACEs is the Lord Jesus Christ, Y'Shua Hamashiach. He is your healer, deliverer, comforter, provider, redeemer and restorer. Then Jesus said, **"Come to me, all of you who are weary and carry heavy burdens, and I will give you rest. Take my yoke upon you. Let me teach you, because I am humble and gentle at heart, and you will find rest for your souls (Matthew 11:28-29).** It doesn't matter what you have faced in life, Come to Jesus! He is your lifeline and will give you rest no matter what ACEs you have experienced past, present and future.

"**And after you have suffered a little while, the God of all grace, who has called you to his eternal glory in Christ, will himself restore, confirm, strengthen, and establish you**" (1 Peter 5:10). Peter encourages the Christians that they do not have to grow weary in the midst of their afflictions. After they have suffered, in other words, they were in need of suffering, but it would not kill them but only be for a little while and the God of all grace will restore them. So whatever ACEs you have had to experience in life, they are only for a little while then the God of all grace and comfort will not only help you to conquer them but restore you back to your original state, confirm that you are called according to his purpose and plan for your life, strengthen you to move past the pain and establish His word in your heart **"Yet in all these things we are more than conquerors through Him who loved us (Romans 8:37).** There is also no shame in needing help to conquer ACEs whether through Biblical counseling, therapy, addiction groups or even medical assistance. Do not let pride keep you from asking for help but trust God to lead you on the right path to your complete freedom! He did it and continues to do it for me and I know He will do it for you!

F.A.I.T.H. – Forsaking All I Trust Him
RESOURCES

Alcoholics Anonymous – *www.aa.org*

Alcoholics Anonymous 24 Hour Hotline – 510.839.8900 (English) 510.502.8560 (Spanish)

Anger Management – National Crime Prevention Council – *www.ncpc.org*

Anxiety and Depression Association of America – *www.adaa.org/supportgroups*

Celebrate Recovery – *www.celebraterecovery.com*

Child Abuse/Neglect Hotline - Virginia: 1.800.552.7096, Out-of-State: 804.786.8536

Crisis Call Center – *www.hopeline-nc.org*, 1.919.231.4525

Narcotics Anonymous – *www.na.org*

National Alliance on Mental Health – *www.nami.org/Find-Support*

National Domestic Violence Hotline – 1.800.799.7233

National Suicide Prevention Lifeline – 1.800.273.8255

Prevent Domestic Violence – *www.awpdv.org*

Recovery Centers of America – *www.recoverycentersofamerica.com/alcohol/anonymous*

Suicide Prevention Services of America - *www.spsamerica.org*

Teen Challenge USA – *www.teenchallengeusa.com*

The Holy Bible – New International Version

ENDNOTES

https://www.ncbi.nlm.nih.gov/pubmed/9635069/Accessed October 2017

https://www.inspirationpeak.com/cgi-bin/stories.cgi?record=50/Accessed October 2017

https://www.nveee.org/statistics/2016/Accessed October 2017

https://www.childtrends.org/wp-content/uploads/2014/07/Brief-adverse-childhood-experiences_FINAL.pdf/Accessed October 2017

https://grassrootschange.net/2015/07/growing-the-aces-movement-to-prevent-and-recognize-adverse-childhood-experiences/Accessed October 2017

https://www.intouch.org/read/steps-to-forgiving-others/Accessed October 2017

F.A.I.T.H. – Forsaking All I Trust Him

TO ORDER MORE COPIES

For order information go to **www.alite4life.com**

THANK YOU!

F.A.I.T.H. JOURNAL

A journal is a private book or diary used to record your ideas, experiences and reflections. Your creativity determines whether you express yourself through words, illustrations, photos, poems, artwork or a combination of expressions. Journaling is an opportunity for you to creatively depict images of your personal story, thoughts and feelings. This F.A.I.T.H. Journal is designed to help you to grow in your relationship with God. As you pray, listen for God's voice and visually see answered prayer as this activates your faith. Record your experiences so you can see and be able to share tangible evidence with others of how God answered your prayers then encourage them to create their own F.A.I.T.H. Journal.

Your F.A.I.T.H. Journal expresses your very own personality based upon your experiences, thoughts, feelings and what you are hearing God say and do, so feel free to creatively illustrate your conversations and faith journey with God. Your journal entries can include but are not limited to your personal testimonies, bible verses, prayers, sermon notes, poems, quotes, photos, artwork and songs. The next twenty-one pages of this book have been designed for your F.A.I.T.H. Journal. Some experts say that it takes 21 days to break a bad habit or form a new one, my prayer is that at the end of 21 days you will be at a totally new level of faith and will not stop there! Remember this, journaling should be made easy and fun, so don't over-think things or it will become drudgery and you may quit. I am looking forward to hearing how the act of journaling has encouraged you and helped you to keep track of some meaningful F.A.I.T.H. experiences in your life.

MY F.A.I.T.H. JOURNAL

MY F.A.I.T.H. JOURNAL

MY F.A.I.T.H. JOURNAL

MY F.A.I.T.H. JOURNAL

MY F.A.I.T.H. JOURNAL

MY F.A.I.T.H. JOURNAL

MY F.A.I.T.H. JOURNAL

MY F.A.I.T.H. JOURNAL

MY F.A.I.T.H. JOURNAL

MY F.A.I.T.H. JOURNAL

MY F.A.I.T.H. JOURNAL

MY F.A.I.T.H. JOURNAL

MY F.A.I.T.H. JOURNAL

MY F.A.I.T.H. JOURNAL

MY F.A.I.T.H. JOURNAL

MY F.A.I.T.H. JOURNAL

MY F.A.I.T.H. JOURNAL

MY F.A.I.T.H. JOURNAL

MY F.A.I.T.H. JOURNAL

MY F.A.I.T.H. JOURNAL

MY F.A.I.T.H. JOURNAL

MY F.A.I.T.H. JOURNAL

10% OF BOOK PROCEEDS WILL SUPPORT BIG BROTHERS BIG SISTERS, DOMESTIC VIOLENCE CENTERS AND RETURNING CITIZENS

www.ingramcontent.com/pod-product-compliance
Lightning Source LLC
LaVergne TN
LVHW051508070426

835507LV00022B/2999